PIANO • VOCAL • GUITAR

THE COMPLETE

VOLUME ONE • A — I

ARRANGED BY TODD LOWRY

ISBN 0-88188-913-X

HAL•LEONARD®
CORPORATION
7777 W. BLUEMOUND RD. P.O. BOX 13819 MILWAUKEE. WI 53213

CONTENTS

11 Across The Universe

4 Act Naturally

8 All I've Got To Do

16 All My Loving

20 All Together Now

26 All You Need Is Love

31 And I Love Her

34 And Your Bird Can Sing

38 Anna (Go To Him)

43 Another Girl

46 Anytime At All

50 Ask Me Why

56 Baby It's You

61 Baby, You're A Rich Man

64 Baby's In Black

68 Back In The U.S.S.R

72 Bad Boy

77 Ballad Of John And Yoko, The

82 Because

90 Being For The Benefit Of Mr. Kite

96 Birthday

102 Blackbird

85 Blue Jay Way

106 Boys

110 Can't Buy Me Love

117 Carry That Weight

114 Chains

120 Come Together

123 Continuing Story Of Bungalow Bill, The

126 Cry Baby Cry

134 Day In The Life, A

140 Day Tripper

129 Dear Prudence

144 Devil In Her Heart

149 Dig A Pony

154 Dig It

160 Dizzie Miss Lizzie

157 Do You Want To Know A Secret?

164 Doctor Robert

172 Don't Bother Me

169 Don't Let Me Down

178 Don't Pass Me By

187 Drive My Car

190 Eight Days A Week

194 Eleanor Rigby

200 End, The

197 Every Little Thing

206 Everybody's Got Something To Hide Except Me and My Monkey

210 Everybody's Trying To Be My Baby

217 Fixing A Hole

222 Flying

225 Fool On The Hill, The

228 For No One

234 For You Blue

238 From Me To You

242 Get Back

244 Getting Better

231 Girl

248 Glass Onion

252 Golden Slumbers

255 Good Day Sunshine

258 Good Morning Good Morning

263 Good Night

266 Got To Get You Into My Life

270 Happiness Is A Warm Gun

276 Hard Day's Night, A

288 Hello, Goodbye

292 Help!

281 Helter Skelter

296 Her Majesty

298 Here Comes The Sun

310 Here, There And Everywhere

314 Hey Bulldog

318 Hey Hey Hey Hey

326 Hey Jude

330 Hold Me Tight

303 Honey Don't

321 Honey Pie

338 I Am The Walrus

334 I Call Your Name

343 I Don't Want To Spoil The Party

348 I Feel Fine

351 I Me Mine

354 I Need You

358 I Saw Her Standing There

364 I Should Have Known Better

368 I Wanna Be Your Man

374 I Want To Hold Your Hand

378 I Want To Tell You

382 I Want You (She's So Heavy)

371 I Will

386 I'll Be Back

390 I'll Cry Instead

397 I'll Follow The Sun

394 I'll Get You

405 I'm A Loser

400 I'm Down

408 I'm Happy Just To Dance With You

412 I'm Looking Through You

420 I'm Only Sleeping

417 I'm So Tired

424 I've Got A Feeling

434 I've Just Seen A Face

431 If I Fell

438 If I Needed Someone

446 In My Life

442 Inner Light, The

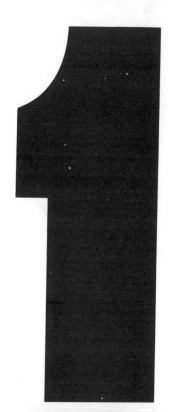

ACT NATURALLY

Words and Music by
VONIE MORRISON and JOHNNY RUSSELL

ev- er hit the big - time. And all I got - ta do is

act nat - 'ral - ly.

We'll

ALL I'VE GOT TO DO

Words and Music by JOHN LENNON
and PAUL McCARTNEY

ACROSS THE UNIVERSE

Words and Music by
JOHN LENNON and PAUL McCARTNEY

Words are flow-ing out__ like end-less rain__ in-to a pa-per cup,__ they slith-er while__ they pass, they slip a-way__ a-cross the un-i-verse.__ Pools of sor-row, waves of joy are drift-ing through my o-pened mind,__ pos -

ALL MY LOVING

Words and Music by
JOHN LENNON and PAUL McCARTNEY

you,_____ All___ my lov-ing,___ dar-

-ling, I'll___ be true._____

end (or bridge + back)

To Coda

no chord

E bar then back to C#m (x2)

ALL TOGETHER NOW

Words and Music by
JOHN LENNON and PAUL McCARTNEY

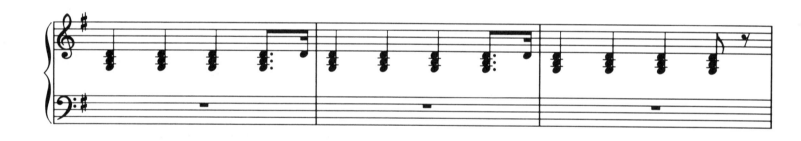

One, two, three, four, can I have__ a-

22

CODA

G

(3 times, gradually getting faster)

All to-geth - er now, (All to-geth-er now) All to-geth - er

now, (All to-geth-er now) All to-geth - er now, (All to-geth-er now)

1,2 G   3 D7

All to-geth - er now, (All to-geth-er now) All to - geth - er

G

now.

ALL YOU NEED IS LOVE

Words and Music by
JOHN LENNON and PAUL McCARTNEY

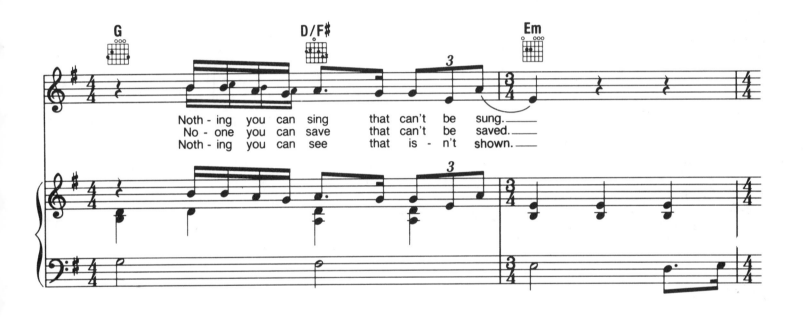

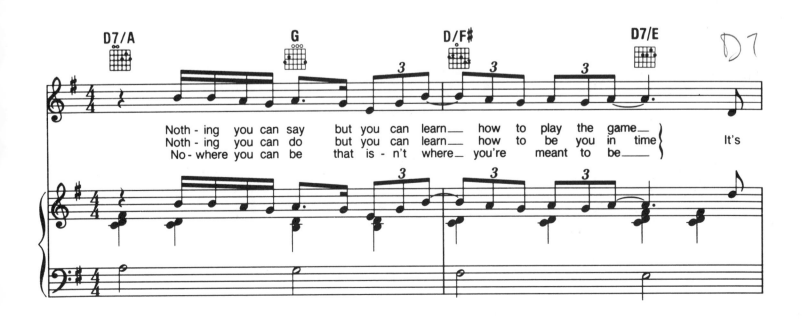

AND I LOVE HER

Words and Music by JOHN LENNON
and PAUL McCARTNEY

AND YOUR BIRD CAN SING

Words and Music by
JOHN LENNON and PAUL McCARTNEY

Tell me that you've got ev-'ry-thing you want,
You say you've seen sev-en won-ders,

and your bird can sing, but you don't get me,___
and your bird is green, but you can't see me,___

you don't get me.
you can't see me.

36

ANNA (GO TO HIM)

Words and Music by
ARTHUR ALEXANDER

42

ANOTHER GIRL

Words and Music by
JOHN LENNON and PAUL McCARTNEY

day, well, I've__ got some-bod - y that's new. I ain't__ no
all the world__ can do what__ she can do. And so__ I'm
day, well, I've__ seen some-bod - y that's new. I ain't__ no

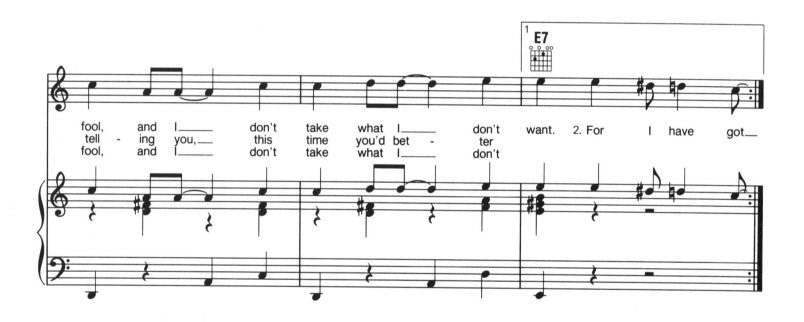

fool, and I____ don't take what I____ don't want. 2. For I have got__
tell - ing you,__ this time you'd bet - ter
fool, and I____ don't take what I____ don't

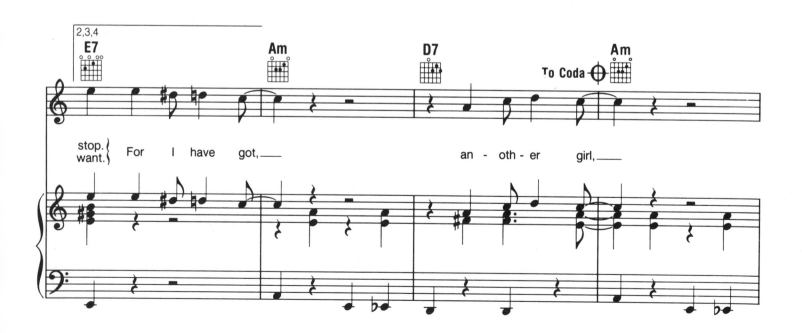

stop. For I have got,____ an - oth - er girl,____
want.

ANYTIME AT ALL

Words and Music by
JOHN LENNON and PAUL McCARTNEY

An-y-time_ at all,_____ an-y-time_ at all,_____ an-y-time_ at all,_____ all_ you got-ta do is call,_____ and I'll_ be there.

To Coda

48

ASK ME WHY

Words and Music by JOHN LENNON
and PAUL McCARTNEY

I love you, _____

_____ 'cause you tell me things I want to know. _____

And it's true _____ that it real-ly on-ly

53

BABY, IT'S YOU

Words and Music by MACK DAVID,
BURT F. BACHARACH and BARNEY WILLIAMS

Sha la la la la la la.

Sha la la la la la la.

Sha la la la la la la.   Sha la la la

BABY, YOU'RE A RICH MAN

Words and Music by
JOHN LENNON and PAUL McCARTNEY

BABY'S IN BLACK

Words and Music by
JOHN LENNON and PAUL McCARTNEY

though he'll nev-er come back, she's dressed in black.
though it's on-ly a whim, she thinks of him.

Oh, how long will it take till she sees the mis-take she has

made. Dear what can I do? Ba-by's in black and I'm_ feel-ing blue. Tell me

66

BACK IN THE U.S.S.R.

Words and Music by
JOHN LENNON and PAUL McCARTNEY

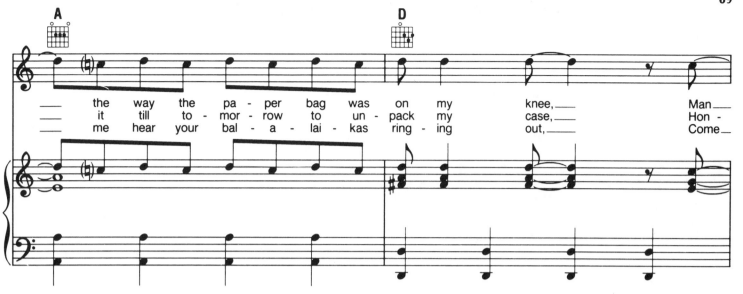

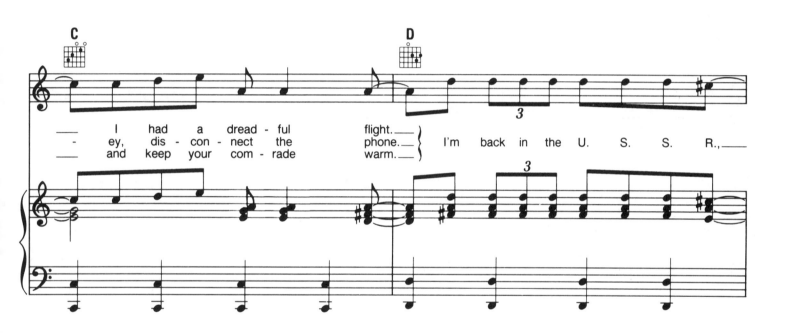

BAD BOY

Words and Music by
LARRY WILLIAMS

Moderate rock and roll

74

rock and roll mu - sic all night._
spin - nin' in a hu - la hoop._
bath in moth - er's laun - dro - mat._

G7

Well he put thumb - tacks on teach - er's chair,
Well his rock and roll has got - ta stop,
Well ya mam - ma said it's got - ta stop,

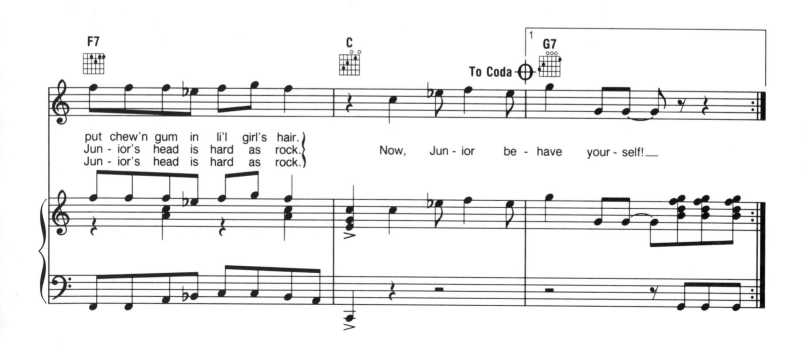

F7   **C**   **To Coda**   **G7**   1

put chew'n gum in li'l girl's hair.)
Jun - ior's head is hard as rock.}
Jun - ior's head is hard as rock.)

Now, Jun - ior be - have your - self!_

have your - self!___ *Ow!*

THE BALLAD OF JOHN AND YOKO

Words and Music by
JOHN LENNON and PAUL McCARTNEY

Moderate rock

1. Stand-ing in the dock at South-amp-ton, trying to get to Hol-land or France. The
2. Final-ly made the plane in-to Pa-ris, hon-ey-moon-ing down by the Seine. The Pe-ter
3. Pa-ris to the Am-ster-dam Hil-ton, talk-ing in our beds for a week. The

man in the mac said, "You've got to go back." You know they
Brown called to say, "You can make it O. K., You can get
news-peo-ple said, "Say, what're you do-ing in bed?" I said, "We're

BECAUSE

Words and Music by
JOHN LENNON and PAUL McCARTNEY

Be - cause the world is round, it turns me
cause the wind is high, it blows my
cause the sky is blue, it makes me

D.S. al Coda

Love is all, love is you.   Be -

CODA

Ah

Ah

Oo   Ah

BLUE JAY WAY

Words and Music by
GEORGE HARRISON

88

Please don't be long,_____ or I may be a - sleep._____

Please don't be long, please don't you

be ver - y long, Please don't be long.

Please don't be long.

BEING FOR THE BENEFIT OF MR. KITE

Words and Music by JOHN LENNON
and PAUL McCARTNEY

late of Pab - lo Fan - que's fair; what a scene.___ O - ver
Mis - ter Kite flies through the ring; don't be late.___ Mes-s'rs
som - er - sets he'll un - der - take on sol - id ground.___ Hav - ing

men and hors - es, hoops and gar - ters, last - ly through a hog's - head of
K. and H. as - sure the pub - lic their pro - duc - tion will be sec - ond to
been some days in prep - a - ra - tion, a splen - did time is guar - an - teed for

real fire.___ In this way Mis - ter K. will chal - lenge the
none.___ And of
all.___ And to

night Mis - ter Kite is top - ping the bill.

BIRTHDAY

Moderately Fast Rock

Words and Music by
JOHN LENNON and PAUL McCARTNEY

You say it's your birth - day,

BLACKBIRD

Words and Music by
JOHN LENNON and PAUL McCARTNEY

Slowly and smoothly

Black - bird sing-ing in the dead of night___
Black - bird sing-ing in the dead of night___

Take these bro - ken wings___ and learn to fly;___
Take these sunk - en eyes___ and learn to see;___

All your life___ you were on - ly wait - ing for this mo - ment to a -
All your life___ you were on - ly wait - ing for this mo - ment to be

BOYS

Moderate rock and roll

Words and Music by LUTHER DIXON
and WES FARRELL

1. I been told when a boy kiss a girl___
2,3. My girl says when I___ kiss her lips___

take a trip a - round the world.___ }
she gets a thrill through her fin - ger - tips.___ } Hey,

CAN'T BUY ME LOVE

Words and Music by
JOHN LENNON and PAUL McCARTNEY

CHAINS

Moderately

Words and Music by GERRY GOFFIN
and CAROLE KING

Chains,_____ my ba - by's got me
Chains,_____ well, I can't break a -

locked up in chains,_____ and they ain't the
way from these chains,_____ can't run a -

kind_____ that you can
round_____ 'cause I'm not

115

CARRY THAT WEIGHT

Words and Music by
JOHN LENNON and PAUL McCARTNEY

119

COME TOGETHER

Moderately slow, with a double-time feeling

Words and Music by
JOHN LENNON and PAUL McCARTNEY

Here come old flat-top, He come groov-ing up slow-ly, He got Joo Joo eye-ball, He one

ho-ly roll-er, He got hair down to his knee.

Got to be a jok-er, He just do what he please.

121

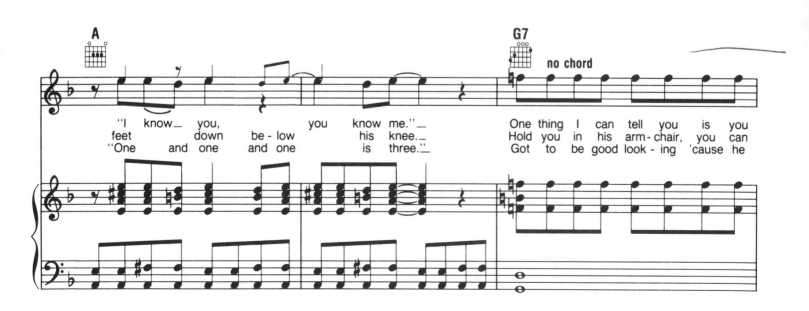

got to be free.
feel his dis-ease. } Come to-geth - er, ___ right now, ___ o - ver me. ___
so hard to see.

Dm7

1,2 | **3**

Repeat and Fade

Come to-ge - ther, ___ Yeah!

THE CONTINUING STORY OF BUNGALOW BILL

Words and Music by JOHN LENNON
and PAUL McCARTNEY

Lyrics (verse):

Hey, Bun-ga-low Bill, what did you kill, Bun-ga-low Bill? Hey, Bun-ga-low Bill what did you kill, Bun-ga-low Bill? He

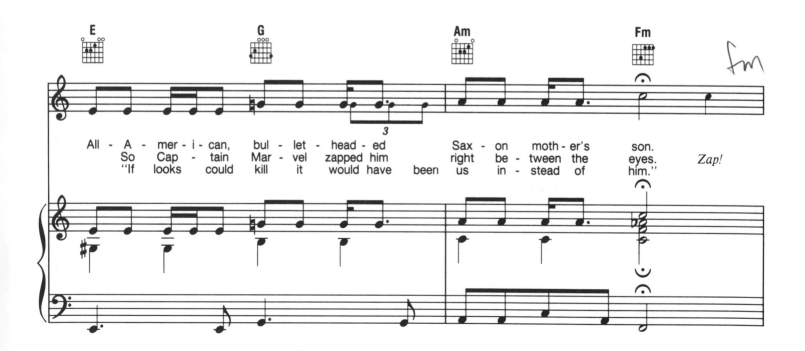

CRY BABY CRY

Words and Music by JOHN LENNON
and PAUL McCARTNEY

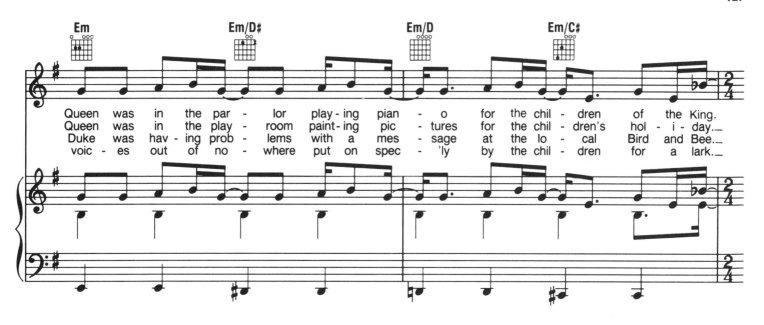

Queen was in the par - lor play-ing pian - o for the chil - dren of the King.
Queen was in the play - room paint-ing pic - tures for the chil - dren's hol - i - day.___
Duke was hav-ing prob - lems with a mes - sage at the lo - cal Bird and Bee.___
voic - es out of no - where put on spec - 'ly by the chil - dren for a lark.___

Cry,___ ba - by, cry,___ make your moth-er sigh.___ She's

old e - nough_ to know_ bet - ter,_____ so cry,___ ba - by, cry,___

(2.) The
(3.) The
(4.) At

DEAR PRUDENCE

Words and Music by
JOHN LENNON and PAUL McCARTNEY

Dear_____ Pru - dence,_
_____ Pru - dence,_
_____ Pru - dence,_

won't you come out   to   play?_____
o - pen   up   your eyes._____
let me see   you   smile._____

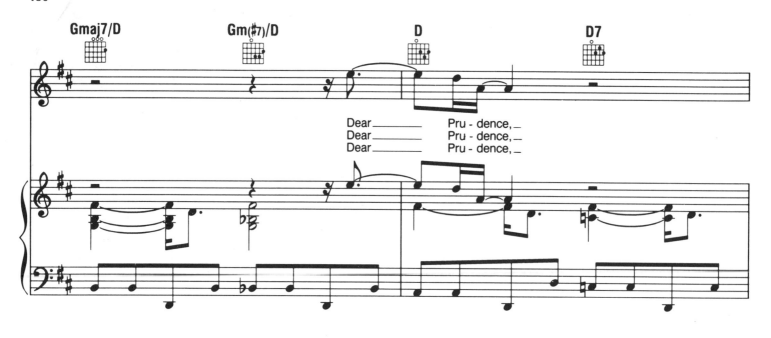

A DAY IN THE LIFE

Words and Music by
JOHN LENNON and PAUL McCARTNEY

135

I read the news to-day oh boy four thou-sand holes in Black-burn

139

DAY TRIPPER

Words and Music by
JOHN LENNON and PAUL McCARTNEY

Moderate Rock

E7

Got a good rea - son   for
She's a big tea - ser,
Tried to please_ her,

DEVIL IN HER HEART

Words and Music by
RICHARD B. DRAPKIN

146

148

DIG A PONY

Words and Music by JOHN LENNON
and PAUL McCARTNEY

want,
are,
see,
Yes, you can cel - e - brate__ an - y -
Yes, you can rad - i - ate__ ev - 'ry -
Yes, you can in - di - cate__ an - y -

thing you want.
thing you are.
thing you see.
Oh,_____
Oh,
Oh, now,
now,

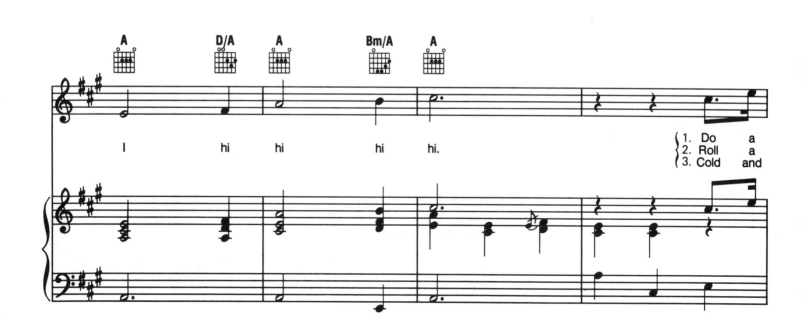

I hi hi hi hi.

1. Do a
2. Roll a
3. Cold and

153

DIG IT

Words and Music by JOHN LENNON, PAUL McCARTNEY,
GEORGE HARRISON and RICHARD STARKEY

155

156

DO YOU WANT TO KNOW A SECRET?

Words and Music by
JOHN LENNON and PAUL McCARTNEY

Slowly and freely

You'll nev - er know how much I real - ly love you,

You'll nev - er know how much I real - ly care.

Moderately

List - en,___

DIZZY MISS LIZZIE

Words and Music by
LARRY WILLIAMS

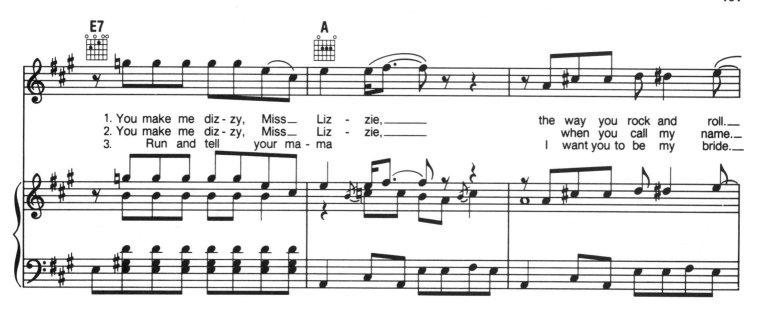

1. You make me diz-zy, Miss__ Liz-zie,_____ the way you rock and roll.__
2. You make me diz-zy, Miss__ Liz-zie,_____ when you call my name.__
3. Run and tell your ma-ma I want you to be my bride.__

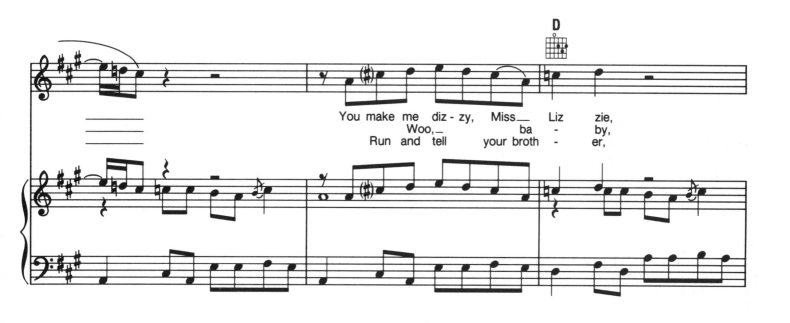

_____ You make me diz-zy, Miss__ Liz zie,
Woo,__ ba - by,
Run and tell your broth - er,

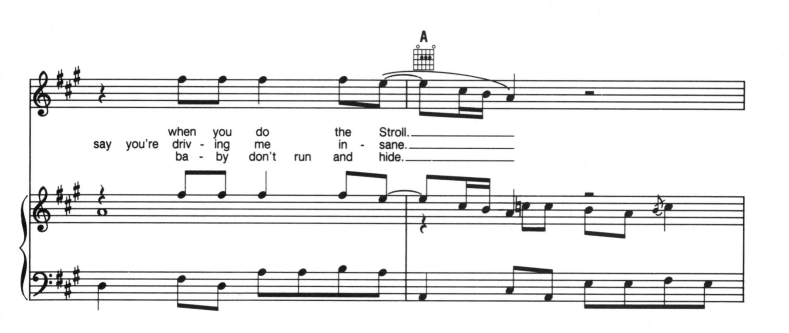

when you do the Stroll._____
say you're driv - ing me in - sane._____
ba - by don't run and hide._____

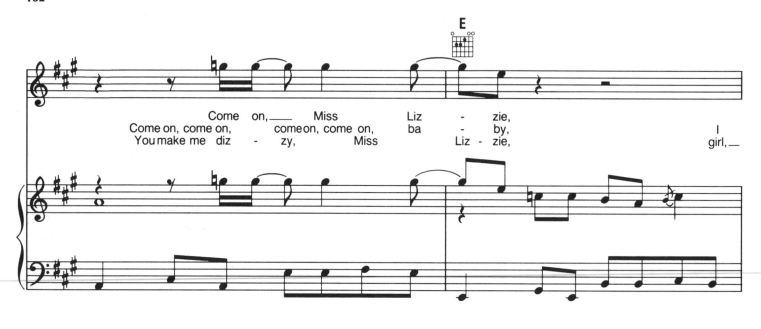

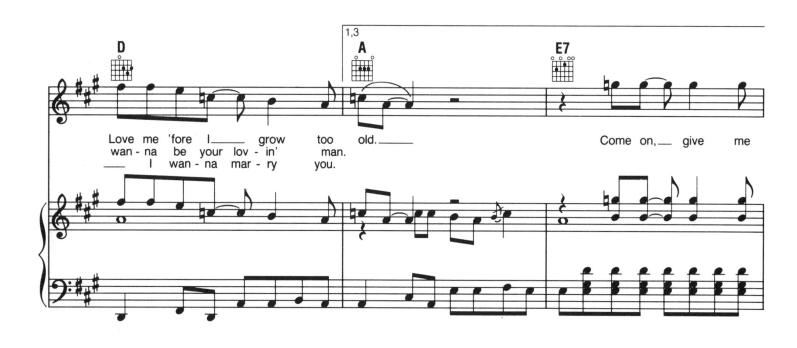

DOCTOR ROBERT

Words and Music by
JOHN LENNON and PAUL McCARTNEY

Ring my friend,__ I said__ you'd call, Doc - tor
If you're down,__ he'll pick__ you up, Doc - tor
My friend works__ for the Na - tional Health, Doc - tor

Rob - ert.
Rob - ert.
Rob - ert.

Day or night,__ he'll be
Take a drink__ from his
Don't pay mon - ey just to

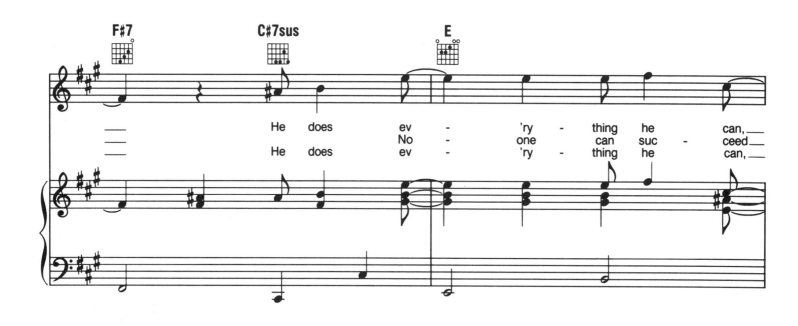

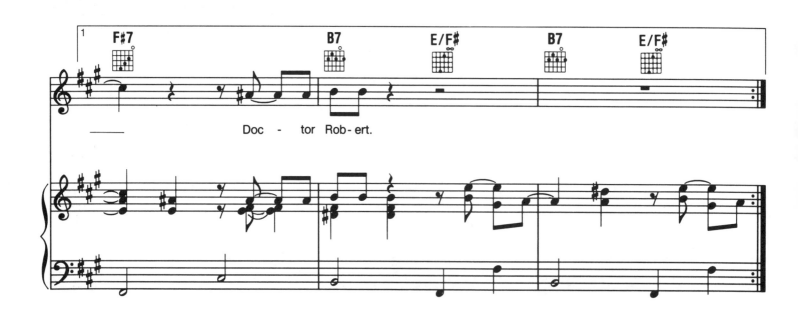

DON'T LET ME DOWN

Words and Music by
JOHN LENNON and PAUL McCARTNEY

DON'T BOTHER ME

Words and Music by
GEORGE HARRISON

To Coda

leave me a - lone, don't both - er me.

Solo

I've got no time

DON'T PASS ME BY

Country style in 2, not too fast

Words and Music by
RICHARD STARKEY

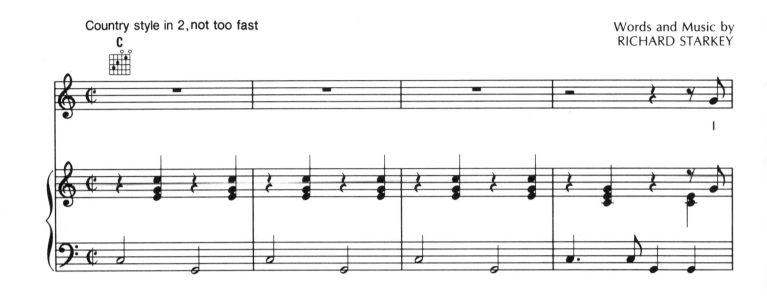

I

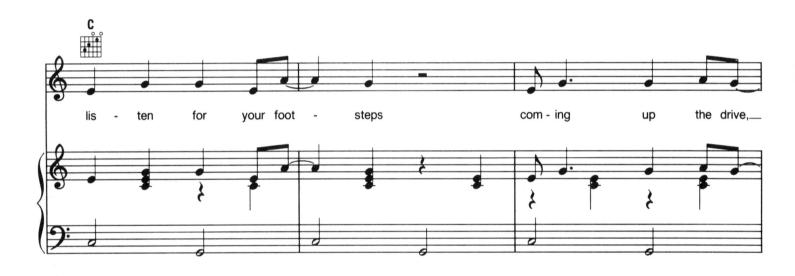

lis - ten for your foot - steps com - ing up the drive,

Lis - ten for your foot - steps,

185

DRIVE MY CAR

Words and Music by
JOHN LENNON and PAUL McCARTNEY

EIGHT DAYS A WEEK

Words and Music by
JOHN LENNON and PAUL McCARTNEY

ELEANOR RIGBY

Words and Music by
JOHN LENNON and PAUL McCARTNEY

195

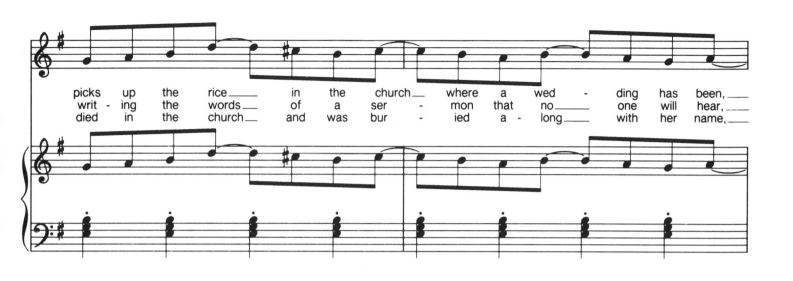

picks up the rice_____ in the church___ where a wed - ding has been,_____
writ - ing the words___ of a ser - mon that no_____ one will hear,_____
died in the church___ and was bur - ied a - long___ with her name,_____

C   Em

_____ lives in a dream._____ Waits at the win - dow,
_____ no one comes near._____ Look at him work - ing,
_____ no - bod - y came._____ Fa - ther Mc Ken - zie,

C

wear - ing the face___ that she keeps___ in a jar___ by the door,___
darn - ing his socks___ in the night___ when there's no - bod - y there,___
wip - ing the dirt___ from his hands___ as he walks___ from the grave,___

EVERY LITTLE THING

Words and Music by
JOHN LENNON and PAUL McCARTNEY

198

THE END

Words and Music by JOHN LENNON
and PAUL McCARTNEY

yeah!   All   right!   Are___ you gon - na be   in   my dreams___

___ to - night?___

Love you, —— love you, ——

204

EVERYBODY'S GOT SOMETHING TO HIDE EXCEPT ME AND MY MONKEY

Words and Music by JOHN LENNON
and PAUL McCARTNEY

Strong rock beat

Come on, come on, come on, come on.

Come on is such a joy. Come on is such a joy.

Come on is take it eas-y. Come on is take it eas-y.
Come on is make it eas-y. Come on is make it eas-y. Take it

EVERYBODY'S TRYING TO BE MY BABY

Words and Music by
CARL LEE PERKINS

Moderate - rock and roll

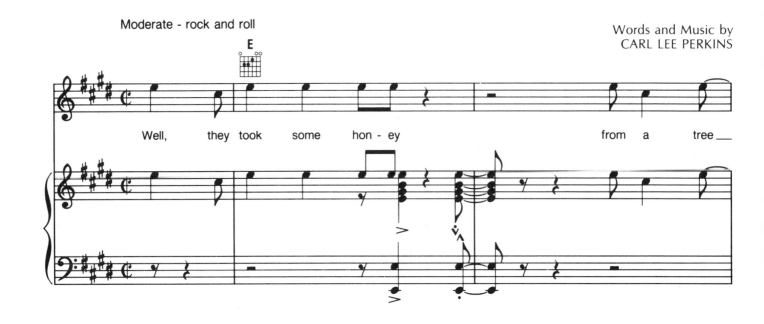

Well, they took some hon-ey from a tree

dressed it up and they called it me. Ev -

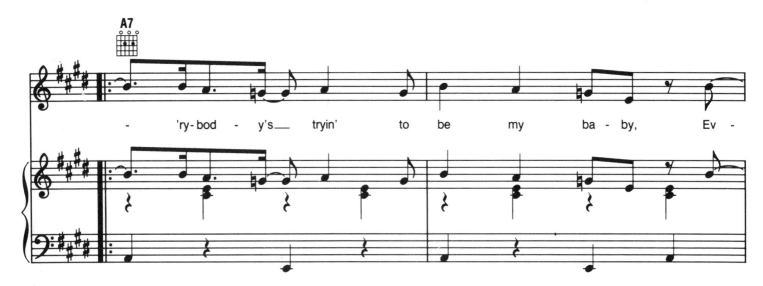

-'ry-bod-y's tryin' to be my ba-by, Ev -

215

FIXING A HOLE

Words and Music by
JOHN LENNON and PAUL McCARTNEY

FLYING

Words and Music by JOHN LENNON, PAUL McCARTNEY,
GEORGE HARRISON and RICHARD STARKEY

THE FOOL ON THE HILL

Words and Music by
JOHN LENNON and PAUL McCARTNEY

FOR NO ONE

Words and Music by
JOHN LENNON and PAUL McCARTNEY

GIRL

Words and Music by
JOHN LENNON and PAUL McCARTNEY

FOR YOU BLUE

Words and Music by
GEORGE HARRISON

235

Be - cause you're sweet and love - ly, girl, it's true.
I want you at the mo - ment I feel blue.
You looked at me, that's all you had to do.

I love you more than ev -
I'm liv - ing ev - 'ry mo -
I feel it now, I hope

- er girl, I do.
- ment girl, for you.
you feel it too.

Be -

(Spoken:) Bop.

Bop   cat   bop.

Go Johnny,   go.

There go the twelve bar   blues___

(Spoken:) Elmore James got nothin' on this baby.

D.S. al Coda

CODA

Give it the blues.

FROM ME TO YOU

Words and Music by
JOHN LENNON and PAUL McCARTNEY

247

GLASS ONION

Words and Music by JOHN LENNON
and PAUL McCARTNEY

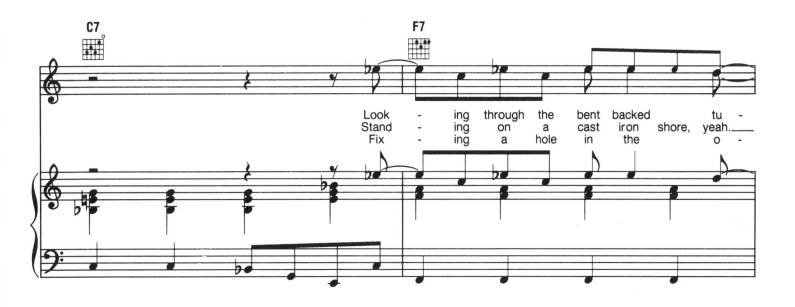

GOLDEN SLUMBERS

253

Good Day Sunshine

Words and Music by
JOHN LENNON and PAUL McCARTNEY

GOOD MORNING GOOD MORNING

Words and Music by JOHN LENNON
and PAUL McCARTNEY

Good morn - ing,— good morn - ing,— good morn - ing,— good morn - ing,— good morn - ing - a.

Noth - ing to do— to save his life,— call his wife in.
Af - ter a while— you start to smile,— now you feel cool.
Some - bod - y needs— to know the time,— glad that I'm here.

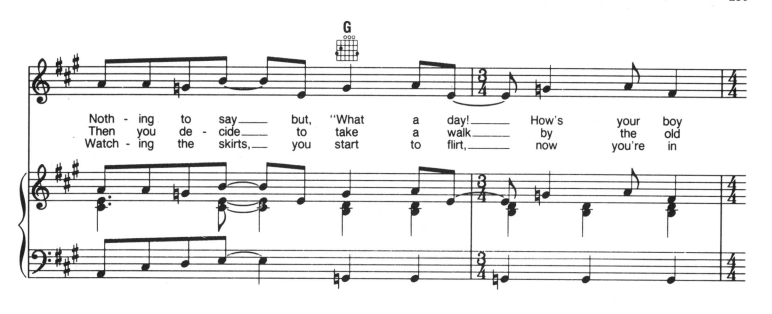

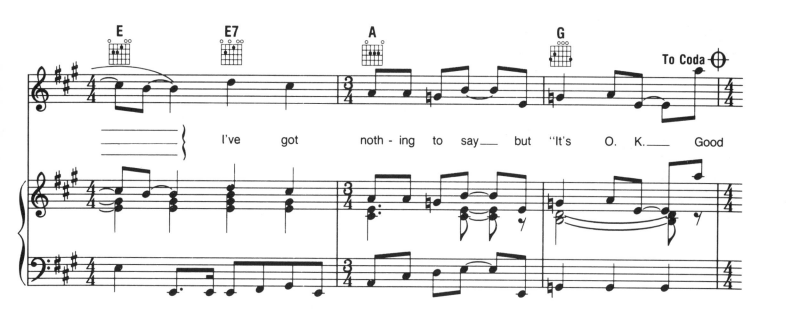

260

ing, Ev - 'ry - thing is closed,___ it's like a ru - in, Ev - 'ry - one you see___ is half a - sleep

___ and you're on your own,___ you're in the street.___

Peo - ple run - ning 'round,___ it's five o'- clock.___

Ev - 'ry - where in town___ it's get - ting dark,___ Ev - 'ry - one you see___ is full of life,___

It's time for tea and meet the wife.

D.S. al Coda

trem.

CODA

morn - ing,___ good morn - ing,___ good.___

Good

GOOD NIGHT

Words and Music by JOHN LENNON
and PAUL McCARTNEY

Lyrics:
Now it's time to say good night; Good night, sleep tight. Now the sun turns out his light;

GOT TO GET YOU INTO MY LIFE

Words and Music by
JOHN LENNON and PAUL McCARTNEY

could see an-oth-er kind of mind there.
we'd meet a-gain for I'd have told you.
and if I do I know the way there.

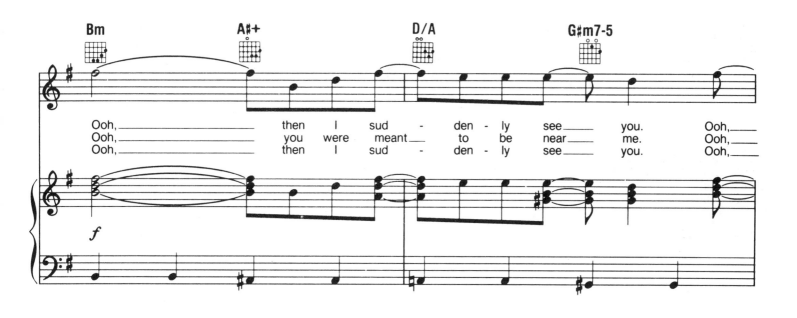

Ooh, then I sud-den-ly see you. Ooh,
Ooh, you were meant to be near me. Ooh,
Ooh, then I sud-den-ly see you. Ooh,

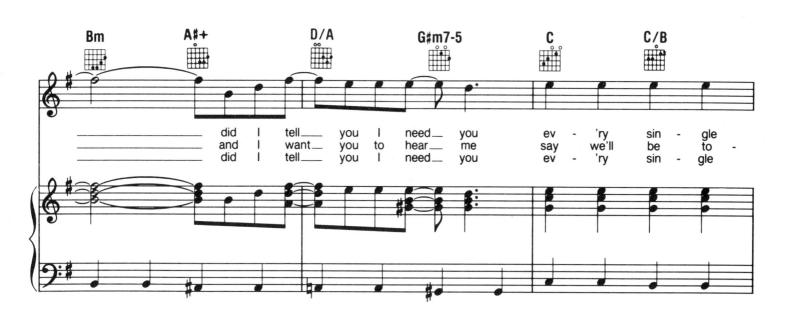

did I tell you I need you ev-'ry sin-gle
and I want you to hear me say we'll be to-
did I tell you I need you ev-'ry sin-gle

268

Got to get you in - to my life!___

Repeat and Fade

HAPPINESS IS A WARM GUN

Words and Music by
JOHN LENNON and PAUL McCARTNEY

Very slowly

She's not a girl who miss-es much,

Du du du du du du Oh, yeah.

She's well ac-quaint-ed with the touch of the vel-vet hand like a liz-ard on a

273

A HARD DAY'S NIGHT

Words and Music by
JOHN LENNON and PAUL McCARTNEY

get home to you____ I find the thing that you do____ will make me

love to come home____ 'Cause when I get you a - lone____ you know I'll

feel__ al - right.____ You know I

be__ O.__ K.____

When I'm home__

ev - 'ry-thing seems to be al-right.

When I'm home__

feel - ing you hold - ing me tight,

tight, yeah, It's been a

HELTER SKELTER

Words and Music by
JOHN LENNON and PAUL McCARTNEY

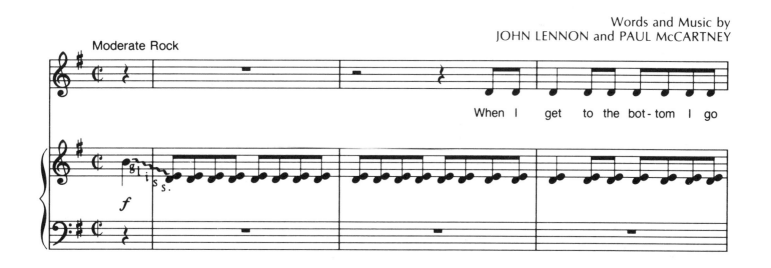

When I get to the bot - tom I go

back to the top of the slide,__ Where I stop and I turn, and I go for a ride,__

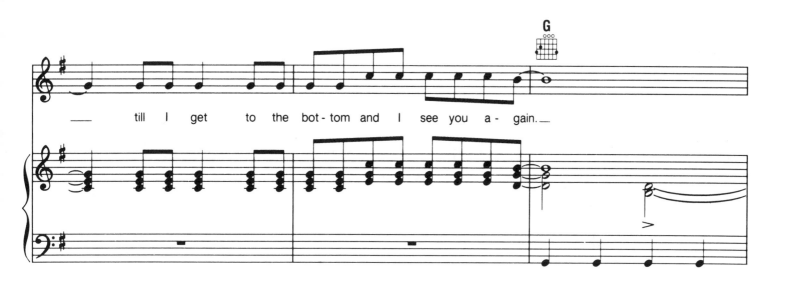

__ till I get to the bot - tom and I see you a - gain.__

Yeah, yeah, yeah,___ yeah.   But

do you, don't you, want___ me to love___ you?   I'm

com-ing down fast but I'm miles a-bove___ you.

Tell me, tell me, tell___ me,   come on tell___ me the an - swer.

Well will you, won't you want___ me to make___ you?
do you, don't you want___ me to make___ you?

I'm com - ing down fast but don't let me break___ you.

Tell me, tell me, tell___

Look out! 'cause here she come!

A   E

A   Em

When I

E7   A/E

get   to the bot-tom, I go back   to the top of the slide,— And I stop and I

HELLO, GOODBYE

Words and Music by
JOHN LENNON and PAUL McCARTNEY

HELP!

Words and Music by
JOHN LENNON and PAUL McCARTNEY

HER MAJESTY

Words and Music by JOHN LENNON
and PAUL McCARTNEY

Her Maj - es - ty's a pret - ty nice girl, but she does - n't have a lot to say.___ Her Maj - es - ty's a pret - ty nice girl, but she chang - es from day___ to day.___

HERE COMES THE SUN

Words and Music by
GEORGE HARRISON

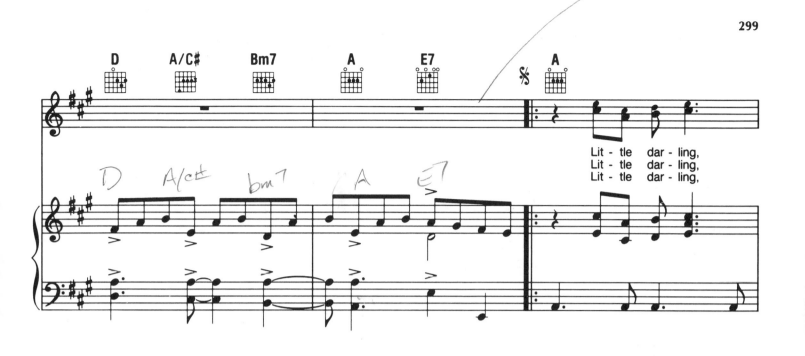

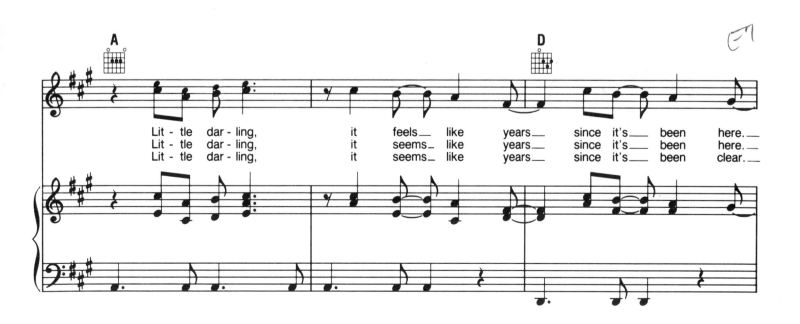

Sun, sun, sun, here it comes.

HONEY DON'T

Words and Music by
CARL LEE PERKINS

(Spoken): I feel fine.

Hum: Mmm hmm.

309

HERE, THERE AND EVERYWHERE

Words and Music by JOHN LENNON
and PAUL McCARTNEY

311

HEY BULLDOG

Words and Music by JOHN LENNON
and PAUL McCARTNEY

Sheep - dog standing in the rain,
Child - like no one un - der - stands,
Big man wait - ing in the dark,

Bull - frog do - ing it a - gain.
Jack - knife in your sweat - y hands.
Wig - wam, fright - ened of the dark.

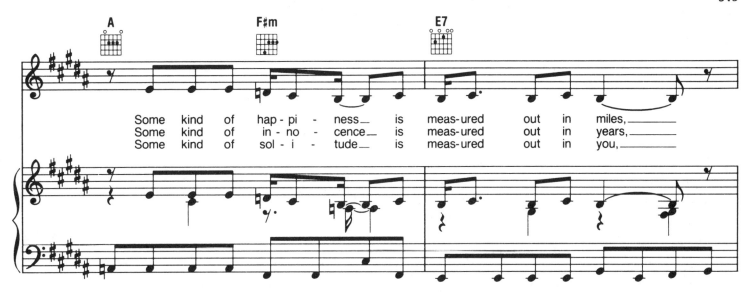

Some kind of hap-pi - ness__ is meas-ured out in miles,_____
Some kind of in-no-cence__ is meas-ured out in years,_____
Some kind of sol - i - tude__ is meas-ured out in you,_____

What makes you think you're some - thing spe - cial when you smile?__
You don't know what it's like to
You think you know me but you

lis - ten to your fears.__
have-n't got a clue.

You can__ talk__ to me,__

HEY HEY HEY HEY

Words and Music by
RICHARD PENNIMAN

HONEY PIE

Words and Music by
JOHN LENNON and PAUL McCARTNEY

HEY JUDE

Words and Music by JOHN LENNON
and PAUL McCARTNEY

HOLD ME TIGHT

Words and Music by JOHN LENNON
and PAUL McCARTNEY

It feels so right now, hold me tight,—
hold me tight,—

tell me I'm the on - ly one,— And
let me go on lov - ing you,— To -

then, I might— nev - er be the
night, to - night,— mak - ing love to

331

I CALL YOUR NAME

Words and Music by JOHN LENNON
and PAUL McCARTNEY

Don't you know I can't

I   call   your   name.__

CODA

Repeat and Fade

I AM THE WALRUS

Words and Music by
JOHN LENNON and PAUL McCARTNEY

Slow 4

I am he as you are he as, you are me and we are all to-geth-
Ex-pert tex-pert chok-ing smok-ers, don't you think the jok-er laughs at you?_

- er_____

See how they run, like pigs from a gun, see how_
See how they smile, like pigs in a sty, see how_

342

I DON'T WANT TO SPOIL THE PARTY

Words and Music by
JOHN LENNON and PAUL McCARTNEY

I don't
want to spoil the par - ty, so I'll go. _____
had a drink or two and I don't care. _____

I would hate my dis - ap - point - ment to
There's no fun in what I do if she's not

D.S. al Coda

Though to-

CODA

I FEEL FINE

Words and Music by
JOHN LENNON and PAUL McCARTNEY

Ba - by's good to me,__ you know,__ she's hap - py as can be,__
Ba - by says she's mine,__ you know,__ she tells me all the time,__
Ba - by says she's mine,__ you know,__ she tells me all the time,__

__ you know,__ she said so.
__ you know,__ she said so.
__ you know,__ she said so.

I ME MINE

Words and Music by
GEORGE HARRISON

I me me mine, _____ I me me mine, _____

____ I me me mine, _____

D.S. al Coda

All _____ through your life, _____ I me mine. _____

I NEED YOU

Words and Music by
GEORGE HARRISON

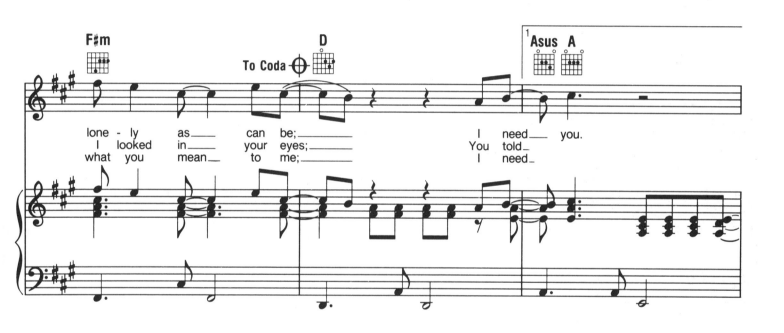

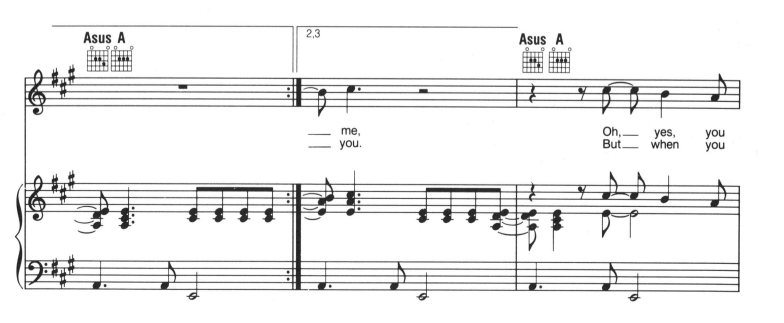

told me   you don't want my lov-in' an-y-more.__
told me   you don't want my lov-in' an-y-more.__

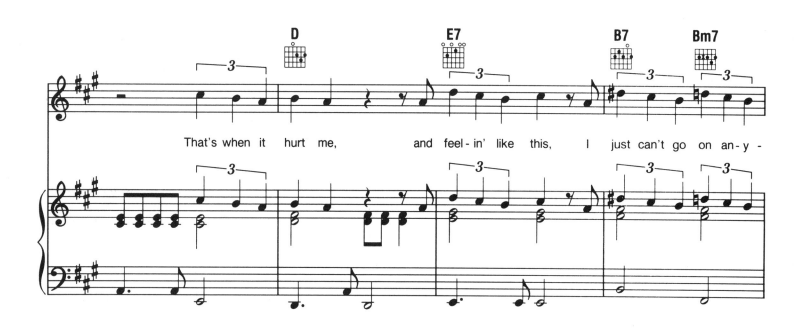

That's when it hurt me,   and feel-in' like this, I just can't go on an-y-

D.S. al Coda

more._____

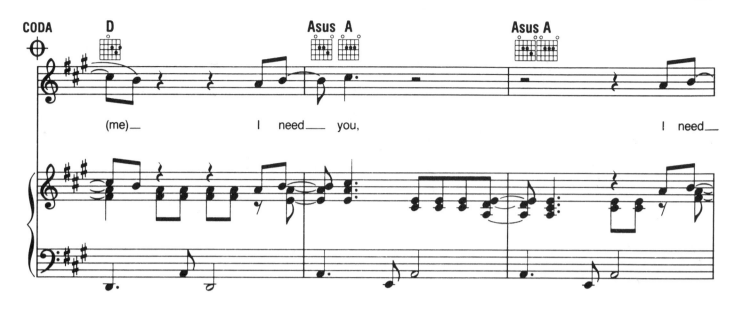

CODA

(me)__ I need__ you, I need__

__ you, I need__ you.

I SAW HER STANDING THERE

Bright Rock

Words and Music by
JOHN LENNON and PAUL McCARTNEY

I SHOULD HAVE KNOWN BETTER

Words and Music by
JOHN LENNON and PAUL McCARTNEY

Moderately

I WANNA BE YOUR MAN

Words and Music by
JOHN LENNON and PAUL McCARTNEY

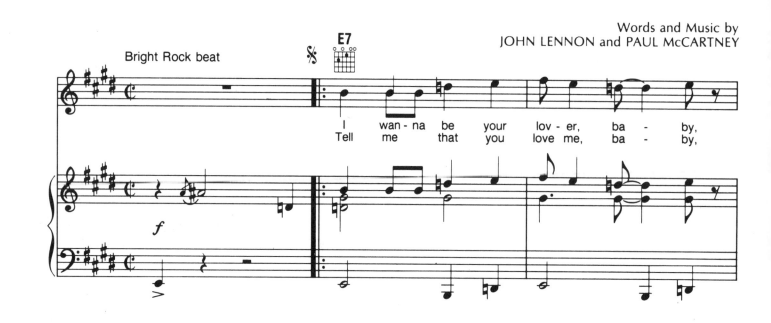

I wan - na be your man, _

I WILL

Words and Music by
JOHN LENNON and PAUL McCARTNEY

373

I WANT TO HOLD YOUR HAND

MCA MUSIC PUBLISHING

376

I WANT TO TELL YOU

Words and Music by
GEORGE HARRISON

I WANT YOU
(SHE'S SO HEAVY)

Words and Music by
JOHN LENNON and PAUL McCARTNEY

I'LL BE BACK

Words and Music by
JOHN LENNON and PAUL McCARTNEY

I'LL CRY INSTEAD

Words and Music by
JOHN LENNON and PAUL McCARTNEY

392

I'LL GET YOU

Moderately

Words and Music by JOHN LENNON
and PAUL McCARTNEY

I'LL FOLLOW THE SUN

Words and Music by
JOHN LENNON and PAUL McCARTNEY

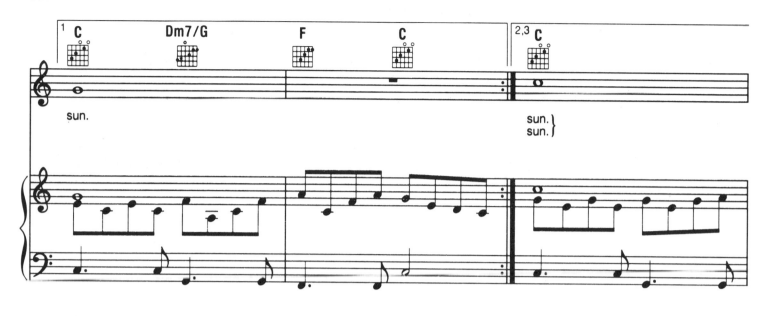

sun.

sun.}
sun.}

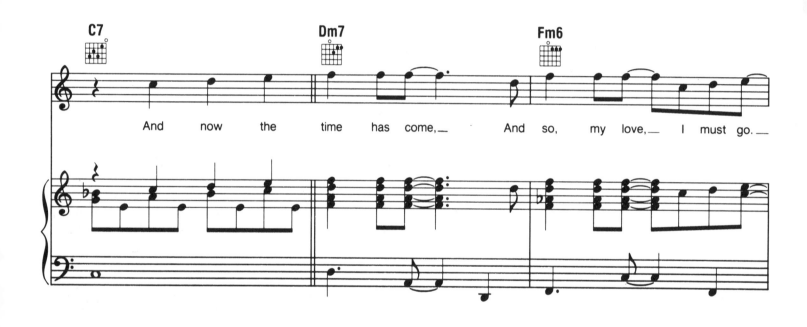

And now the time has come,— And so, my love,— I must go.—

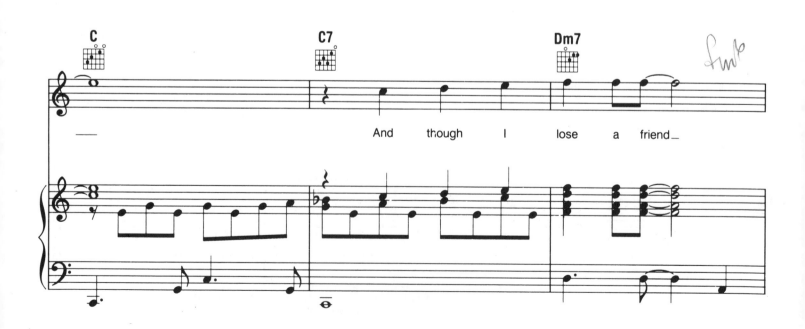

— And though I lose a friend—

I'M DOWN

Words and Music by JOHN LENNON
and PAUL McCARTNEY

A ba- by you know I'm down.

I'M A LOSER

Words and Music by
JOHN LENNON and PAUL McCARTNEY

There is one love_____ I should nev - er have crossed.
Be - neath this mask_____ I am wear - ing a frown._
I re - a - lize_____ I have left it too late._

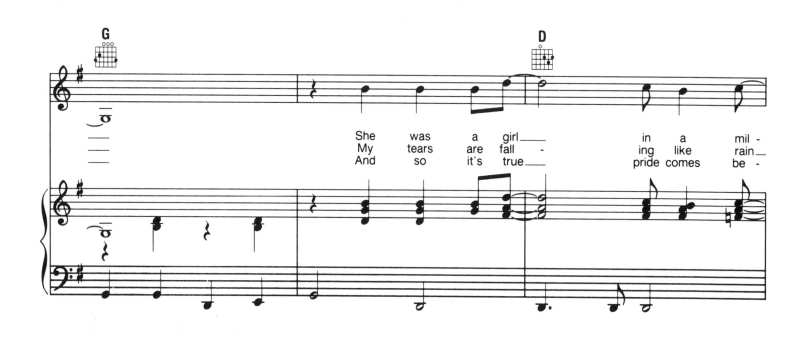

She was a girl_____ in a mil -
My tears are fall - ing like rain_
And so it's true_____ pride comes be -

- lion, my friend._ I should have known_
from the sky_ Is it have for her_
- fore a fall_ I'm tell - ing you_

I'M HAPPY JUST TO DANCE WITH YOU

Words and Music by
JOHN LENNON and PAUL McCARTNEY

Be - fore this dance is through,— I think I'll love you too,— I'm so hap - py when you dance with me. I don't

want to kiss or hold your hand,—
need to hug or hold you tight,—

If it's
I just

I'M LOOKING THROUGH YOU

Words and Music by
JOHN LENNON and PAUL McCARTNEY

I'm look-ing through____
Your lips are mov-

____ you, where did you go?____
-ing, I can-not____ hear.

415

I'M SO TIRED

Words and Music by JOHN LENNON
and PAUL McCARTNEY

420

I'M ONLY SLEEPING

Words and Music by
JOHN LENNON and PAUL McCARTNEY

I'VE GOT A FEELING

Words and Music by JOHN LENNON
and PAUL McCARTNEY

I've got a feel - in', a feel - in' deep in - side,
Oh, please be - lieve me, I'd hate to miss the train,
I've got a feel - in', that keeps me on my toes,

oh, yeah.
oh, yeah,
oh, yeah,

(2nd) yeah,

oh, yeah.
oh, yeah.
oh, yeah.

oh,   no.
oh,   no.
oh,   yeah.

Yeah,

yeah,   I've got a feel - in',   yeah.

To Coda ⊕

(2nd) I've got a feel - in'.

All   these   years I've been

Ev - 'ry bod - y saw the sun shine.___
Ev - 'ry - bod - y put their

foot down.___

oh no.___

IF I FELL

Words and Music by
JOHN LENNON and PAUL McCARTNEY

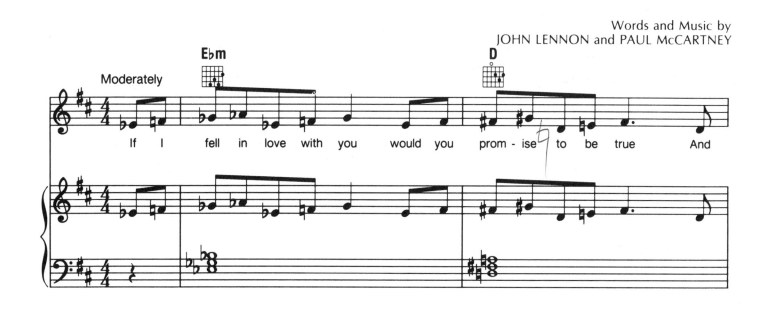

If I fell in love with you would you prom-ise to be true And

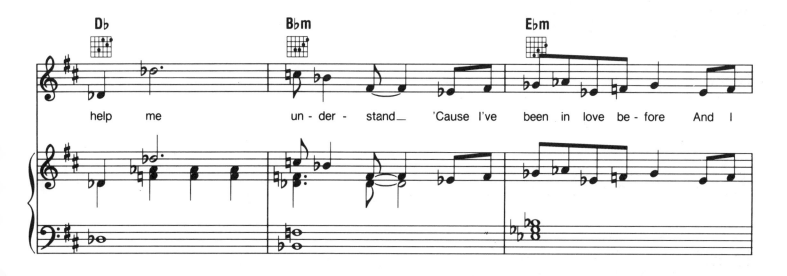

help me un-der-stand__ 'Cause I've been in love be-fore And I

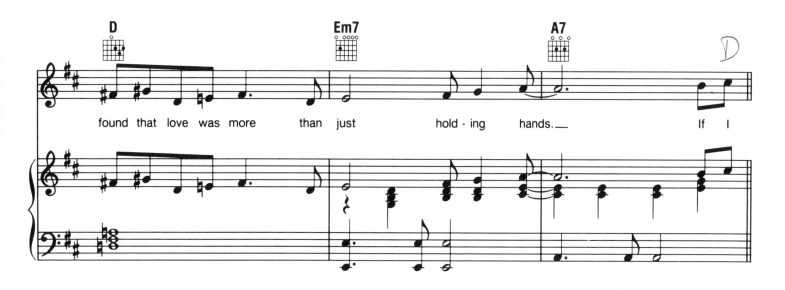

found that love was more than just hold-ing hands.__ If I

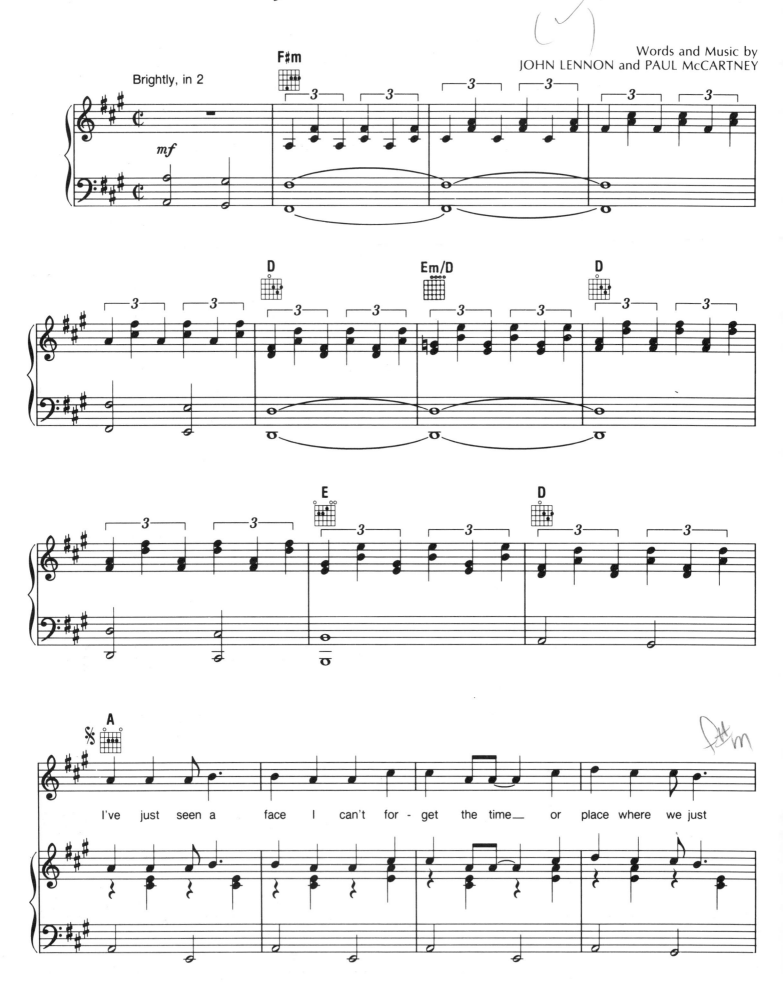

I'VE JUST SEEN A FACE

Words and Music by
JOHN LENNON and PAUL McCARTNEY

Brightly, in 2

I've just seen a face I can't for- get the time____ or place where we just

IF I NEEDED SOMEONE

Moderately

Words and Music by
GEORGE HARRISON

If I need-ed some-one to love,
If I had-ed some more time to spend,

you're the one that I'd be think-ing of,
then I guess I'd be with you, my friend.

If I need-ed some-one.
If I need-ed some-one.

Had you come some oth - er day, then it might not have been like this, But you see now I'm too much in love.

THE INNER LIGHT

Words and Music by
GEORGE HARRISON

With -

444

IN MY LIFE

Words and Music by
JOHN LENNON and PAUL McCARTNEY